TRINIDAD &

THE UPDATED TRAVEL GUIDE

Discover the Mystery of TrinBago: The Ultimate Holiday Guide to Discover the Best of the Sights, Experiences, and Luxury of the Land of the Hummingbird.

John Schnell

TABLE OF CONTENTS

INTRODUCTION

As the plane descended into Piarco International Airport, my excitement grew exponentially. Trinidad and Tobago, a twin-island nation nestled in the southern Caribbean, had always beckoned to me with promises of vibrant culture, stunning landscapes, and warm hospitality. This was the beginning of my much-anticipated journey to explore the treasures of these two captivating islands.

Touching down in Trinidad, the rhythmic beat of steel drums welcomed me to the lively atmosphere that permeates the island. From the vibrant street life of Port of Spain to the lush landscapes of the Northern Range, every corner of Trinidad seemed to pulsate with energy. My first stop was the Queen's Park Savannah, a vast green expanse encircling the city, where locals gathered for picnics, jogged along the track, and engaged in spirited games of cricket. The surrounding historic mansions and the iconic Queen's Royal College provided a picturesque backdrop to this lively urban oasis.

Immersing myself in the local culture, I made my way to the Maracas Bay, renowned not only for its golden sands but also for the legendary bake and shark shacks lining the shore. As I indulged in this culinary delight—freshly caught shark stuffed into warm, doughy bread—the crashing waves provided a soothing soundtrack to the feast. The authenticity of the experience was underscored by the friendly banter of locals and the vibrant hues of the fishing boats bobbing in the bay.

With a heart full of Trinidad's vivacity, I hopped on a short flight to Tobago, where a different rhythm awaited. The smaller of the two islands, Tobago promised a more laid-back atmosphere and pristine natural beauty. My first glimpse of the coastline took my breath away—the azure waters lapping against the powdery white sands painted a scene straight from a postcard.

Venturing into the Main Ridge Forest Reserve, the oldest protected rainforest in the Western Hemisphere, I embarked on a guided hike. The trail led me through a lush canopy alive with the chatter of exotic birds and the occasional rustle of wildlife. Emerging at the lookout point, I was greeted by the panoramic view of the Caribbean Sea—a sight that left me in awe of Tobago's untouched landscapes.

Exploring the coastal villages, I discovered Speyside, a charming fishing community renowned among diving enthusiasts. Here, I donned snorkeling gear and descended into the waters of Buccoo Reef, a kaleidoscopic underwater world teeming with vibrant coral formations and an array of marine life. The Nylon Pool, a shallow sandy area surrounded by crystal-clear waters, provided the perfect spot for a refreshing swim, completing an aquatic adventure that felt like a dream.

As the sun dipped below the horizon, I couldn't resist the allure of Tobago's legendary Sunday School in Buccoo. Contrary to its name, this weekly street party was a celebration of life, music, and dance. Locals and visitors alike gathered under the open sky, moving to the infectious beat of soca and calypso tunes. The vibrant colors of the traditional costumes, the aroma of local delicacies, and the warmth of the people created an atmosphere of pure jubilation.

In Trinidad and Tobago, I found a perfect balance—a yin and yang of pulsating energy and serene tranquility. From the bustling streets of Port of Spain to the untouched beauty of Tobago's beaches, each moment unfolded as a unique chapter in a captivating story. As I boarded the plane for my departure, the rhythm of the islands echoed in my heart, leaving me with memories of an unforgettable journey in this Caribbean paradise.

WELCOME TO TRINIDAD AND TOBAGO

Location and Geography

The southernmost islands in the West Indian Island chain that divides the Atlantic and Caribbean seas are Trinidad and Tobago. 5,128 square kilometers make up the territory of Trinidad (1,980 square miles). The Gulf of Praia, which is between seven and twenty miles wide, divides it from Venezuela.

It is located northeast of Venezuela, between 10° and 11° north of the Equator. It is a geographical extension of the continent of South America. Trinidad, the bigger island, is 50 miles long and 35 to 45 miles broad.

From east to west, Trinidad is traversed by three relatively modest mountain ranges, with the thickly wooded Northern Range reaching the maximum height of 3,085 feet. A third range runs down the southern shore, while a lower range crosses the island's center laterally. Trinidad offers a diverse range of tropical flora and fauna.

Tobago is located 116 square miles, 21 miles northeast of Trinidad. With altitudes reaching 1,800 feet, the topography is mostly rough; the only significant lowland is a coral platform near the southwest end.

Weather and Climate

Due to its near proximity to the equator, Trinidad and Tobago experiences two distinct seasons due to different climatic types.

Different dry and wet season regimens set these seasons apart. The tropical marine climate that is representative of the dry season, which runs from January to May, is marked by warm days and mild nights, moderate to strong low level winds, and primarily showery rainfall from midday convection.

The wet season, which runs from June to December, is represented by a modified moist equatorial environment with low wind speeds, hot, humid days and nights, and a noticeable increase in rainfall, largely due to migratory and latitudinal changing equatorial weather systems. It is believed that late May and December mark the beginning of the rainy and dry seasons, respectively.

The main causes of the differences in the two climatic seasons between the islands of Trinidad and Tobago are their respective sizes, orographies, elevations, trade wind orientations, and geographic locations.

The hurricane season, which occurs from June to November and peaks in August and October, is a part of the rainy season. Due to its physical position, Trinidad is on the southern edge of the hurricane basin in the North Atlantic. As a result, storms do not directly reach Trinidad as often as they do Tobago; yet, the weather in the surrounding areas is comparable to that of Tobago due to the passage of tropical storm systems.

The daily temperature cycle in Trinidad and Tobago is more noticeable than the seasonal one. With an average daily temperature of 26.5 degrees Celsius, the long-term mean annual maximum and lowest temperatures are 31.3 and 22.7 degrees Celsius, respectively.

The rainy season is often warmer than the dry season, with March being the hottest month during the dry season and September being the warmest month during the wet season.

Trinidad has more annual and seasonal rainfall than Tobago; nonetheless, both islands' rainfall patterns exhibit a unique bi-modal behavior, with early (June) and late (November) rainy season maxima. The main rainfall season in Trinidad is June, whilst the main season in Tobago is November.

A Concise History of Trinidad and Tobago

The history of the islands of Trinidad and Tobago is rich and complicated, formed by many cultures, colonial conflicts, and a spirit of perseverance. Let's examine the important events that have shaped this unique country as we go into their chronology.

Prior to Colonization:

Indigenous Origins: Indigenous communities lived in Trinidad and Tobago long before European settlers arrived. Archaeological evidence from Tobago suggests human existence there as early as 5000 BC, while the Cedros site in Trinidad shows dwellings that date back 7,000 years.

These prehistoric peoples, who were mostly *Arawakan* and *Carib* peoples, created complex societies, advanced agricultural techniques, and distinctive customs.

Spanish Encounters: Christopher Columbus claimed Trinidad for Spain when he arrived there in 1498. However, the absence of easily accessible resources and Indigenous communities' resistance originally hindered Spanish colonization ambitions. Spanish conquistadors mostly used the islands as a rest stop on their way to South America.

Colonial Era:

Shifting Hands: In the course of European power battles in the 17th and 18th centuries, Trinidad and Tobago was used as pawns. Spain, Britain, France, the Dutch, and even a Latvian trading corporation traded the islands.

Africans who had been forced into slavery at this time were mostly employed on sugarcane plantations.

British Dominance: Britain became the leading colonial power by the early 19th century. With its rapidly growing sugar industry, Trinidad rose to prominence. Tobago, however, continued to be less economically relevant and was transferred more often. The two islands were formally combined into one British colony in 1889.

During the British colonial era, Africans under slavery were brutally exploited. The islands' social fabric was severely damaged by their forced labor, which also contributed to the expansion of the sugar industry. Trinidadian society is still shaped by the history of slavery.

Road to Independence: In Trinidad and Tobago, anti-colonial movements gained traction in the 20th century. The war for independence was fuelled by political agitation, labor discontent, and a developing sense of national identity.

After gaining independence from Great Britain on August 31, 1962, Trinidad and Tobago became a sovereign member of the Commonwealth.

Post-Independence: Trinidad and Tobago has had a number of difficulties after gaining its independence, such as social inequality, political unrest, and economic diversification. But the country has also advanced significantly in the areas of healthcare, education, and cultural advancement.

Trinidad and Tobago's republican status in 1976 was a step closer to self-determination. The country is now a multiethnic, multicultural democracy with influences from Indigenous peoples, Europe, Asia, and Africa.

People and Culture

The development of Trinidad and Tobago culture has been impacted by several civilizations. The many cultures of Indian, African, Portuguese, Amerindian, Spanish, Chinese, and others have a significant impact on Trinidad and Tobago's culture.

The nation's culture has been greatly influenced by its ties to the United Kingdom, and English is the primary language spoken there. The histories and cultures of Trinidad and Tobago and the many regions within the nation also vary significantly from one another.

Here, we examine several fundamental facets of Trinidad and Tobago's culture and social mores:

Trinidad and Tobago's Religion

The three main faiths of Trinidad and Tobago are Islam, Hinduism, and Roman Catholicism. Some of the lesser religious organizations in the nation include the Anglicans, Sikhs, Jews, Buddhists, Presbyterians, Methodists, Traditional African Religion, Taoism, etc.

In Trinidad and Tobago, the Yoruba/Orisha religion, the Spiritual Baptist faith, and two Afro-Caribbean syncretic faiths are the fastest growing religious communities.

American-style evangelical and fundamentalist churches are becoming more and more common throughout the nation.

Trinidad and Tobagoan Music

The music genre known as *calypso* developed in Trinidad and Tobago and is an essential component of the country's culture. It is an Afro-Caribbean musical genre that migrated from the nation to Venezuela and other Caribbean countries. Its beginnings may be attributed to the 18th-century entrance of African slaves accompanied by French colonists.

The *Soca* music genre, which combines calypso with Indian music and rhythms, is another one that originated in Trinidad and Tobago.

Another distinctive musical genre in the nation is *chutney*, which is a blend of Soca and Indian influences. *The Rapso* is a 1970s blend of Calypso and Soca that originated from the nation's socioeconomic instability.

In Trinidad & Tobago, a fusion of Caribbean and Latin American music styles gave rise to *Parang*. Another kind of song that uses words from Trinidadian Hindi and English is called *pichakaree*.

SOME INTERESTING REASONS WHY EVERYONE SHOULD VISIT TRINIDAD AND TOBAGO

Here are some fascinating facts about Trinidad and Tobago that may convince you to pay a visit:

It is renowned for housing the **world's spiciest chili pepper**. The *Moruga Scorpion* pepper boasts a heat rating of 1.2 million Scoville heat units (SHUs), as confirmed by experts from New Mexico State University's Chile Pepper Institute, making it the most potent chili pepper globally.

This pepper contains an equivalent amount of capsaicin, the chemical compound responsible for the burning sensation in peppers, as a shot glass filled with law enforcement-grade pepper spray.

Curious about its effects? Spare yourself the discomfort and observe the bravado of Pepper Heads who dare to try it first.

Named after its place of origin, the southern village of Moruga, this pepper is also linked to the landing site of Christopher Columbus.

Trinidad and Tobago can be credited for the **origin of the limbo**, a beloved classic at parties for both energetic tweens and spirited middle-aged revelers. Rooted in the country's African heritage, the limbo involves dancers passing beneath a stick, sometimes set on fire, at heights as low as 22 cm above the ground.

Home to the **world's largest natural deposit of asphalt**, *the La Brea Pitch Lake* in southwest Trinidad holds approximately 10 million tons of asphalt. Recognized informally as the eighth natural wonder of the world, the lake is one of only three known asphalt deposits globally.

Spanning 109 acres, visitors can walk on its surface as it hisses and bubbles. The asphalt extracted from the lake is used for pavements and runways worldwide. Some claim that the small pools of water forming on the surface during the rainy season have healing properties due to their high sulfur content.

Trinidad and Tobago boasts remarkable biodiversity, hosting around 2,200 species of flowering plants, 400 bird species, 100 mammal species, 85 reptile species, and 30 amphibian species.

It also claims the highest number of bird species per square mile, including 17 types of hummingbirds.

Trinidad's *Grande Riviere* beach witnesses the **second-largest turtle nesting globally**, occurring between March and September. Unfortunately, a botched construction project in 2012 led to the death of thousands of baby turtles.

Diving underwater reveals the **world's largest brain coral**, the *Kelleston Drain*, in Trinidad and Tobago, measuring an impressive 4.9 meters wide.

While Trinidad is renowned for wildlife watching, Tobago offers diverse opportunities as well, with the *Tobago Main Ridge Forest*

Reserve, established in 1776, being the **oldest protected rainforest in the Western Hemisphere.**

The steel pan, a musical instrument crafted from metal parts like paint pots, oil drums, and biscuit tins, originated in Trinidad and Tobago. Developed in the 1930s and continuing to evolve, it is the only new acoustic instrument to emerge in the 20th century, now recognized as a national instrument.

In 1977, *Janelle Commissiong*, a 24-year-old from Trinidad and Tobago, became the **first black Miss Universe**.

Trinidad and Tobago has produced **globally acclaimed figures** in various fields, including cricket legend *Brian Lara* and pop sensation *Nicki Minaj*, who moved to the USA at the age of five.

The largest celebration of Divali in the Western Hemisphere takes place in Trinidad and Tobago. Known as the "*Festival of Lights*," this Hindu religious festival involves the entire population in prayer, reenactments, and the lighting of deyas (clay lamps) symbolizing the triumph of light over darkness and the return of Rama from exile.

Tobago is home to the **world's largest single brain coral colony**, measuring 10 feet (3 meters) high and 16 feet (5.3 meters) across, offering a majestic underwater world for divers.

Trinidad and Tobago are renowned as **the best Caribbean destination to witness Leatherback Turtles**, with over 10,000 of these giants visiting the shores annually. In 2015, Time magazine named Trinidad and Tobago the best place globally to observe Leatherback Turtle hatchlings.

VISA REQUIREMENTS

Citizens of most countries do not need a visa to visit Trinidad and Tobago for tourism or business purposes for a stay of up to 90 days. However, there are a few exceptions, including citizens of countries such as Cuba, Iran, Iraq, North Korea, and Syria. These citizens will need to obtain a visa in advance.

To apply for a visa to Trinidad and Tobago, you will need to submit the following documents:

A completed visa application form

A valid passport

A recent passport-size photograph

A letter of invitation from a friend or relative in Trinidad and Tobago (if applicable)

Proof of financial support (bank statements, etc.)

A medical certificate

A copy of your return ticket

You can apply for a visa at the Trinidad and Tobago embassy or consulate in your home country. The processing time for a visa is usually around two weeks.

Once you have obtained your visa, you will need to present it to immigration officials upon arrival in Trinidad and Tobago. You will also be charged a visa cost.

Here are some additional things to keep in mind when traveling to Trinidad and Tobago:

You must have a valid passport that is valid for at least six months after your intended date of departure from Trinidad and Tobago.

A return ticket or evidence of further travel is required.

You must have sufficient funds to cover your stay in Trinidad and Tobago.

You must be in good health.

If you are planning to travel to Trinidad and Tobago, it is important to check with the Trinidad and Tobago embassy or consulate in your home country for the latest visa requirements.

For Stays Longer than Ninety Days:

Business or Study Visa: You must apply for the necessary visa at the closest Trinidad and Tobago High Commission or Embassy if you want to remain for more than ninety days for business or study. For comprehensive information, it is preferable to get in touch with the appropriate embassy directly since the particular criteria and application procedure may differ.

Other Visa Categories: Nationals of several nations may need visas for purposes other than travel or education, such employment, marriage, or long-term stay. Once again, the best course of action is to get in touch with the Trinidad and Tobago High Commission or Embassy in your nation.

Remember that while the details in this book are correct as of the time of publication, laws and rules regarding visas are subject to change.

It is advisable to verify the most recent prerequisites well in advance of your journey with the Trinidad and Tobago Immigration Division or your closest embassy/high commission.

GETTING TO TRINIDAD AND TOBAGO

It is important to plan ahead for the journey's navigation before you reserve your hammock and snorkel. Let's examine the several routes you may use to go to these beautiful islands:

Flights:

Without a question, flying is the most practical and best alternative for most tourists. It's easy to travel to Trinidad and Tobago from major cities in North America, South America, and Europe thanks to direct connections.

The primary entry point into the islands is Trinidad's *Piarco International Airport* (POS), which serves flights operated by American Airlines, United Airlines, Caribbean Airlines, JetBlue, and British Airways.

Tobago's Arthur Napoleon Raymond Robinson International Airport (TAB): Consider flying straight here to get to Tobago's paradise more quickly. Airlines that provide dedicated flights to the island include Condor and Caribbean Airlines.

By Sea:

Cruise Ships: Choose a cruise that stops in Trinidad and Tobago to start an opulent journey. With this option, you may take advantage of the luxurious facilities of a cruise ship while exploring many Caribbean locations. Several cruise lines provide itineraries that include the islands, including *Carnival Cruise Line* and *Royal Caribbean*.

Ferry: Taking a ferry to Trinidad and Tobago from wherever you are in the Caribbean might be an affordable and scenic option.

From nearby islands including Grenada, St. Vincent, and Guyana, services are provided. *SuperFast Galicia* and *Trinidad and Tobago Fast Ferry* are reputable providers of dependable and enjoyable connections.

Considerations for Choosing Your Travel Method:

Budget: Ferries are the most cost-effective choice; flights are often the most costly. The cost of a cruise might vary based on the ship and itinerary selected.

Time: Ferries take longer but provide a more distinctive travel experience; flights are the quickest method to get to the islands.

Convenience: Take into account the simplicity of layovers and connections while selecting your method of transportation. If convenience is your first priority, direct flights or cruises can be better.

Getting Around Trinidad and Tobago

The most convenient way to navigate Trinidad and Tobago is by car, and you can rent one at either *Trinidad's Piarco International Airport* (POS) or *Tobago's Arthur Napoleon Raymond Robinson International Airport* (TAB). Alternatively, if your exploration is limited, affordable taxis are a viable option.

Buses are also in operation, but they tend to be unreliable. When traveling between islands, head to the docks in Port of Spain or Scarborough and board one of the private ferries.

Car

In Port of Spain, Trinidad, taxis and walking are reliable modes of transportation. However, if you plan to visit Tobago, renting a car is essential, given that the island's transportation infrastructure is less developed.

When renting, opt for a vehicle with four-wheel-drive, as the roads can be challenging. Inquire about auto insurance, as driving styles on both islands tend to be more assertive than what you may be accustomed to.

Taxi

Taxis resemble regular passenger cars but are identifiable by license plates starting with the letter "H." While you can hail a cab at your hotel, fares may be higher.

Instead, wait at designated taxi stands or flag one down on the street. Since taxis lack meters, agree on a fare before entering the vehicle. Most one-way trips typically cost around $1 USD.

Bus

Trinidad's major cities are served by the *Public Transport Service Corporation,* operating bus routes with no fixed timetable. Travelers can also use route taxis, which follow specific paths.

Tickets are available at most bus terminals, but drivers do not accept cash or credit cards. Tobago also has an inexpensive but unreliable bus service, with routes starting at Scarborough's bus terminal and running to Crown Point, Plymouth, and various villages on the island from 6 a.m. onwards.

Ferry

For inter-island travel, the Port Authority of Trinidad and Tobago provides express ferries. The journey takes just under three hours, with a one-way fare costing approximately $8 USD.

Alternatively, a more economical conventional ferry service is available for about $6 USD, but the trip duration is nearly six hours. Trinidad's ferry dock is in Port of Spain, while Tobago's is in Scarborough.

Passengers with vehicles should check in three hours before sailing; otherwise, two hours in advance is sufficient.

SOME CULTURAL ETIQUETTES AND CUSTOMS

To fully appreciate the richness of this experience, it's crucial to familiarize yourself with local etiquette and customs.

So, before you pack your dancing shoes and steel pan spirit, let's explore the nuances of Trinbagonian life:

Greetings and Interactions:

Embrace warmth: Offering a friendly smile and a hearty "*good morning,*" "*good afternoon,*" or "*good evening*" is customary when greeting anyone, be it shopkeepers or fellow travelers.

Show respect with titles: Demonstrating courtesy includes addressing elders as "*Mr./Mrs./Miss*" and authorities as "*Officer*" or "*Doctor.*"

Enjoy liming: "*Liming*" entails leisurely socializing and relishing conversation. Embrace the unhurried pace and avoid rushing interactions.

Respect personal space: Trinbagonians typically maintain a closer personal space, so don't be surprised if your conversation partner stands closer than you're used to.

Table Manners and Dining:

Value invitations: Accepting an invitation for a home-cooked meal is considered a privilege. Arrive on time and bring a small gift, such as flowers or wine, to express appreciation.

Communal dining: Sharing food in a communal style is common, so feel free to try a bit of everything.

Politely refuse food: If you decline something due to dietary restrictions, offer a brief explanation with a thank you.

Leave the napkin on the table: Unlike some cultures, refrain from tucking your napkin into your shirt.

Dressing and Social Decorum:

Appropriate beach attire: Show respect for local sensibilities by wearing beachwear only in designated areas. Dress more modestly when visiting religious sites or rural villages.

Follow footwear etiquette: Shoes are typically removed upon entering homes, so observe cues from your host.

Mind public displays of affection: Public smooching and PDA are generally considered inappropriate.

Be mindful of noise: Loud talking or boisterous behavior in public spaces is discouraged.

Religious and Cultural Nuances:

Respect diverse faiths: Trinidad and Tobago embraces a multi-religious society, so respect various customs and rituals you may encounter.

Celebrate Carnival with respect: Immerse yourself in the vibrant colors and infectious energy of Carnival, but be aware of cultural sensitivities when participating in costumes or festivities.

Ask, don't assume: If uncertain about any specific custom or practice, politely inquire rather than making assumptions.

Remember:

Humor prevails: Trinbagonians enjoy humor, so be prepared for playful teasing and witty banter.

Relax and be present: Slow down, embrace the laid-back island time, and savor the moment.

Cultural exchange is mutual: Share your own cultural insights and be open to learning new things.

IMPORTANT EVERYDAY WORDS YOU SHOULD KNOW

When visiting Trinidad and Tobago, it's helpful to familiarize yourself with some important everyday words and phrases commonly used in the country.

English is the official language of Trinidad and Tobago, but you'll also encounter some local words and phrases influenced by the country's diverse cultural heritage. Here are some keywords to understand:

Liming: This term refers to hanging out, socializing, or relaxing with friends or family. It's a popular concept in Trinidad and Tobago, emphasizing the laid-back and enjoyable aspects of spending time together.

Bess: Derived from the word "*bless*," this term is used to describe something that is good, great, or enjoyable. For instance, you may say, "*This food is bess*!" meaning the food is delicious.

Trini: Short for "*Trinidadian*," this word is used to refer to someone from Trinidad and Tobago. It's also used to describe the local culture, traditions, and dialect.

Bacchanal: This term refers to a lively, often chaotic, or scandalous situation or event. It can also be used to describe playful banter or gossip.

Doh mind: Derived from "*don't mind,*" this phrase is used to tell someone not to worry or bother about something. For example, if someone apologizes for being late, you might respond with "*Doh mind, it's all right.*"

Doubles: A popular Trinidadian street food, doubles consists of two flatbreads called "*bara*" filled with curried chickpeas, chutney, and various condiments. It's a must-try dish when visiting.

Roti: Another delicious Trinbagonian dish, roti is a type of bread usually made from flour and filled with curried meat, vegetables, or other savory ingredients. It's often eaten with various sauces or chutneys.

Palance: This word refers to having a good time, usually at a party or event. It can also mean dancing energetically or enjoying oneself with enthusiasm.

Scene: In Trinidad and Tobago, "*scene*" refers to a gathering or event, often with music, dancing, and socializing. For instance, "*There's a big scene happening downtown tonight.*"

Sweetbread: Unlike the traditional sweetbread made from dough, in Trinidad and Tobago, sweetbread refers to a popular baked bread-like cake that is sweet, rich, and often filled with fruits and nuts. It's commonly enjoyed during festive occasions.

Other Words You Should Know

All right, alright - an expression of agreement or understanding

All now so - Currently, now, at this time

All yuh - all of you

Ansah - answer

Awright - all right

Bawling - crying

Breadfruit - a starchy fruit that is a staple food in Trinidad and Tobago

Bully beef - canned corned beef

Cacao - the seed of the cacao tree, from which chocolate is made

Carnival - a major festival in Trinidad and Tobago that takes place every February

Chaguanas - a Trinidad and Tobago town

Choke - to strangle or suffocate

Cyar - cannot

Dal - lentil

Dhalpuri - a flatbread made from lentils

Farallones - a group of small islands off the coast of Trinidad

Fattie - a large, fat person

Flood - to overflow

Gairy - a nickname for Eric Williams, the first Prime Minister of Trinidad and Tobago

Good food - delicious food

Gros Michel - a type of banana that is the most common variety in Trinidad and Tobago

Hard ears - stubborn

Irie - a word used to express happiness or satisfaction

Jumbie - a ghost or spirit

Laventille - a neighborhood in Port of Spain, Trinidad

Licks - a beating or whipping

Long time no see - a greeting used to express surprise at seeing someone after a long time

Machel - a nickname for Machel Montano, a Trinidadian soca musician

Mamaguy - a trick or deception

Maracas - a town in Trinidad and Tobago that is known for its steel pan music

Mas - a type of masquerade or street performance that is popular during Carnival

Matura - a type of fruit that is similar to a mango

Na - no

Nyuh - you

Oildown - a traditional Trinidadian dish made with meat, vegetables, and dumplings

Pan - a type of steel drum that is used to play soca music

Parang - a type of Christmas music that is popular in Trinidad and Tobago

Pelau - a rice dish that is popular in Trinidad and Tobago

Pholourie - a type of fritter that is popular in Trinidad and Tobago

Port of Spain - Trinidad and Tobago's capital

Red - a popular color in Trinidad and Tobago

Rice and peas - a traditional Trinidadian dish made with rice and pigeon peas

Soca - a type of music that is popular in Trinidad and Tobago

Steel pan - a type of musical instrument that is made from oil drums

Sweet - delicious

Trinbagonian - a person from Trinidad and Tobago

Veggie - a vegetable

Wuk - to work

Yuh – you

Remember that this list is not exhaustive, but it should give you a good starting point for understanding and engaging with locals in Trinidad and Tobago.

PACKING LIST AND ESSENTIALS

Before you start adding bikinis and rum bottles to your suitcase, let's create a thorough list to ensure you're well-prepared for any surprises this lively archipelago may throw your way.

Clothing Essentials:

Beach Basics: Ensure you have 3-4 swimsuits, quick-drying cover-ups, breathable shirts and shorts, and a versatile beach hat. Swimwear dries rapidly under the tropical sun, allowing you to pack light.

Include beach necessities like a towel, a sarong (which can double as a blanket or scarf), your preferred snorkel and mask, and a good book for sun-filled relaxation.

Island Chic: Bring casual sundresses, breezy linen pants, and comfortable tank tops for exploring towns, markets, and local eateries. Include one or two dressier outfits for fancy dinners or nights out.

Footwear: Pack versatile sandals for the beach and walks, sturdy walking shoes for rainforest exploration, and comfortable flip-flops for leisure around your accommodation.

Rain or Shine: Be prepared for sudden tropical downpours with a lightweight rain jacket or a foldable umbrella.

Sun and Fun Essentials:

Sun Protection is Key: Include high-SPF sunscreen (30+ SPF) for both UVA and UVB protection, a wide-brimmed hat, and sunglasses. Opt for reef-safe sunscreen to preserve the islands' underwater ecosystems.

Personal Care: Pack essential toiletries, medications, and insect repellent to ward off mosquitoes. Consider biodegradable mosquito repellent for responsible travel.

Tech and Travel Companions:

Connectivity: Bring a universal adapter for charging devices (the country uses 115V outlets with two flat prongs) and a portable charger for on-the-go power.

Capture the Memories: Remember your camera (preferably waterproof for water activities), extra batteries, and a waterproof phone case for worry-free beachside photos.

Island Tunes: Load your playlist with calypso, soca, and island beats to immerse yourself in the local vibe. Download offline maps and travel apps for navigation without relying on data roaming.

Additional Must-Haves:

Reusable Water Bottle: Stay hydrated in the tropical heat with a reusable water bottle to minimize plastic waste.

First-Aid Kit: Include a basic first-aid kit for minor cuts, scrapes, or headaches.

Snacks for Savvy Travelers: Pack granola bars, dried fruits, or nuts for quick energy boosts. Local markets also offer plenty of delicious snacks.

Small Denominations: Keep small bills in the local currency (Trinidad and Tobago Dollar) for tipping, buying souvenirs, or enjoying street food.

Tips:

Get a heads-up on the weather for your trip and pack what you'll need.

Opt for a light, versatile suitcase to ease your island hopping adventures.

Leave some space in your suitcase for the souvenirs and local handicrafts you'll undoubtedly fall in love with!

HEALTH AND SAFETY
ADVICE

Here's what you should be aware of to ensure your safety in Trinidad and Tobago.

Crime Hot Spots in Trinidad and Tobago:

A general safety guideline for Trinidad and Tobago is to explore during the day and carry a mobile phone for emergencies. Consider purchasing a local sim card if your phone is unlocked.

Certain areas in the capital, Port of Spain, such as *Laventille*, *Morvant*, *Sea Lots*, and *South Belmont*, are known for violent crimes like sexual assault, robberies, and gang violence and should be avoided. *Queen's Park Savannah*, a large park, may be lonely on weekdays and travelers could be targets for theft.

However, during carnival events and weekends, it is generally safe with a food fair offering Trinidadian delicacies.

Avoid seeking out remote beaches like *Englishman's Bay*, *Las Cuevas*, and *King Peter's Bay*, especially at night, as travelers are often targeted for sexual assault or robberies.

Most visits to Tobago are trouble-free, with incidents of violent crime being rare.

Accommodation Safety:

When renting a villa or apartment, ensure there are security measures like burglar bars on windows, outdoor security lighting, and 24-hour security guards. Make sure all doors and windows in your accommodation can be locked securely.

Airport Scams:

Airports can be hotspots for criminals taking advantage of tired visitors. Travelers have been followed from the airport to downtown Port of Spain and even to their accommodation, then robbed.

If traveling after dark from Trinidad's *Piarco International Airport*, be cautious and consider detouring to a public place if you suspect you're being followed.

Highway Robbery:

Some roads, like *Beetham Highway*, can be dangerous. Criminals may force cars to stop, attempting to rob drivers.

Avoid stopping, don't exit your car, and maneuver around debris if encountered.

Bump and Rob Incidents:

Bump and rob incidents, particularly in *Laventille*, involve thieves causing minor collisions to get drivers to stop, then robbing them.

If this occurs, and your car is still drivable, leave the area before seeking help.

Smash and Grab:

Theft from cars, known as smash and grab, is relatively common. Keep valuables out of sight when leaving them in a parked car.

Traffic Tango:

Driving in Trinidad and Tobago can be chaotic. If renting a car, familiarize yourself with local traffic rules and drive defensively.

Consider using taxis or public transportation in unfamiliar areas.

Stick to Safe Sources of Water:

Opt for bottled water or boil tap water for at least 1 minute before drinking. Avoid ice unless it's made from safe water.

Food Safety:

Prioritize food safety by opting for restaurants and street vendors known for their cleanliness and hygiene. Opt for cooked food, and be cautious with raw fruits and vegetables unless you can peel them yourself.

Travel Insurance:

Invest in travel insurance with adequate medical coverage to protect against unexpected illness or injuries.

Vaccinations:

Check with your doctor or a travel clinic for recommended vaccinations based on your itinerary and health situation.

Bonus Tip:

Download the **TT Safe** app for emergency contact information, safety tips, and real-time updates in Trinidad and Tobago.

SOME COMMON SCAMS
YOU SHOULD KNOW

Although Trinidad and Tobago is generally considered a safe destination for travelers, it's essential to stay vigilant and informed about potential scams and challenges. Here is an in-depth guide to common scams that tourists may encounter in the islands:

Airport and Transportation Scams:

Fake Taxis: Watch out for unauthorized individuals posing as taxi drivers at *Piarco International Airport.*

Stick to official taxi stands or pre-booked transportation to avoid inflated fares or being taken to the wrong destination.

Overcharged Fares: Negotiate fares upfront with taxi drivers, particularly for short trips. Be cautious of potential overcharging, especially at night or in remote areas.

Luggage Tampering: Keep a close eye on your luggage at the airport and throughout your travels. Be wary of strangers offering unsolicited help with baggage, as they may attempt to steal valuables.

Accommodation Scams:

Fake Rentals: Exercise caution when booking accommodation online, especially through unofficial websites. Research reputable agencies and check reviews before making any payments.

Hidden Fees: Be mindful of additional fees not included in the advertised price, such as cleaning charges or resort taxes. Read rental agreements carefully and inquire about potential hidden costs.

Double Booking: Confirm your reservation directly with the accommodation provider to avoid the disappointment of arriving at a double booking situation.

Street and Market Scams:

Pickpockets and Bag Snatchers: Be mindful of your belongings in crowded areas like markets and public transport. Keep valuables close to your body and avoid openly displaying expensive items.

The "Friendly Local": Beware of overly friendly locals offering unsolicited help or information, as they might be attempting to distract you while an accomplice picks your pockets.

The "Broken Item" Scam: Someone may pretend to accidentally bump into you, stain your clothes, and offer to clean them while stealing valuables in the process.

Other Scams to Watch Out For:

Fake Jewelry and Souvenirs: Exercise caution with street vendors selling cheap, imitation jewelry or souvenirs. Inspect items carefully before making any purchases.

Currency Exchange Tricks: Always use authorized currency exchange bureaus and double-check the rates before exchanging money.

The "Lost Child" Scam: Scammers may approach you with a fake story about a lost child, hoping you'll be distracted and hand over your valuables.

Tips for Staying Safe:

Trust your gut: Pay attention to those inner alarm bells. If something gives you a weird vibe, don't ignore. . Walk away from any situation that makes you uncomfortable.

Be vigilant: Keep an eye on your belongings and surroundings, especially in crowded areas.

Don't flash cash: Carry only the money you need for the day and keep your valuables out of sight.

Learn some basic Trinidadian phrases: Knowing a few words like "No, thank you" ("No, thanks") can help you politely decline unwanted offers or assistance.

Report scams: If you encounter a scam, report it to the authorities and warn other travelers.

POPULAR ATTRACTIONS IN TRINIDAD AND TOBAGO

Two islands that have been united to become one country, Trinidad and Tobago, have extremely distinct cultures and natural wonders.

The busier of the two and the most southern of all the West Indian islands is Trinidad, which is located close to Venezuela. The vibrant capital of Port of Spain is home to a diverse population of Europeans, Africans, Amerindians and East Indians in addition to some stunning specimens of colonial and Renaissance-style architecture.

Tobago, Trinidad's smaller sister, is naturally lovely but less developed, though it does have upscale resorts. Here, white sand beaches, reefs, and rainforests make up the main tourist attractions. Snorkeling and diving are particularly good.

Numerous independent tourists are drawn to the islands by their spectacular landscape and unpretentious atmosphere. Both islands are especially well-known for their superb birdwatching, with a variety of avian species from neighboring South America contributing to the rich biodiversity.

Carnival, which takes place in Trinidad and Tobago on the Monday and Tuesday preceding Ash Wednesday, is another well-known event.

Port of Spain, Trinidad

The nation's capital, this thriving economic hub is renowned for both its numerous beautiful examples of colonial-style architecture and a few tourist destinations.

Taking in the architectural features of *Queen's Park Savannah* is one of the most popular things to do in Port of Spain. The expansive green area is dotted with magnificent homes known as the "*Magnificent Seven.*" Admirers of architecture should also go to *Woodford Square's* stunning *Red House Parliament.*

The stunning *Royal Botanic Gardens*, which adjoin the president's opulent mansion, and the *National Museum and Art Gallery*, which has displays on regional art, history, and culture, are both located close to *Queen's Park Savannah.*

Carnival: The most well-known aspect of Port of Spain is definitely its vibrant Carnival. The Monday and Tuesday before Ash Wednesday, the city comes alive with a vibrant fiesta of costumes, limbo contests, and infectious soca and calypso beats.

Maracas Bay, Trinidad

Maracas Bay, surrounded by coconut trees, is one of the most well-known beaches in Trinidad. The beautiful 40-minute trip from Port of Spain offers stunning vistas of verdant peninsulas protruding into the sea as you travel through a mountainous jungle.

The beach is among the most exquisite beaches in the vicinity of the city. This perfect crescent of golden sand is lapped by a deep blue bay, and at its outskirts rise lushly covered slopes.

In addition to food trucks and merchants selling delicious foods along the beach, such as the beloved local restaurant *Richard's Bake & Shark*, you may hire chairs and umbrellas to make your beach time more pleasant. There are also showers accessible.

This is a fantastic option if you're seeking for activities in Trinidad where you can spend the day and experience the local culture. One of the most well-liked spots to "lime" in Trinidad is here, where locals prefer to hang around and take in the atmosphere.

About fifteen minutes from Maracas Bay, gorgeous *Las Cuevas Beach* is calmer and less crowded if you're looking for a more laid-back beach day. This is also a great option for families because to the calmer seas.

Nylon Pool, Tobago

Situated near Pigeon Point, the distinctive Nylon Pool offers a swimming experience that will never be forgotten. Situated in the ocean, it has waist-high water that is so clear that guests can see all the way to the supple white coral foundation.

Because of its ideal swimming conditions and tranquil location, this natural pool is among the top tourist destinations in Tobago. From Pigeon Point and Store Bay, it is conveniently accessible by boat.

Families will love the shallow, warm, and clear water at Nylon Pool. The experience of standing in the midst of the ocean will be thrilling for everybody, and children will particularly like the glass bottom boat excursion.

Princess Margaret christened Nylon Pool after her 1962 honeymoon there. The term came from her perception that the clear properties of the water resembled nylon. Since then, it has developed into a very popular romantic spot for local couples.

Argyle Falls, Tobago

The tallest waterfall in Tobago is called Argyle Falls. This radiant cascade, which descends 54 meters, is serene and lovely. The Argyle River inspired the name of the falls, which terminate in deep, crystal-clear pools of water.

How to Get There: From *St. Paul* on the east side of Tobago, travelers must go 1.2 miles on a simple route to reach the falls. This rainforest route may take twenty minutes or more to explore, depending on your walking speed. Walkers will come across some of the most exquisite flora and animals in the region, such as butterflies and kingfishers, throughout the route.

You'll understand the journey was worthwhile after you've arrived. Visitors of all ages will find great relaxation in the tranquil sound of the cascading water, and a cool pool swim is a nice treat.

Fort King George & the Tobago Museum, Tobago

Constructed in the 1780s with a view of *Scarborough Bay*, *Fort King George* stands as one of Tobago's most revered historical tourist destinations and is also the best maintained fort on the island.

With its lush grass, huge ancient trees, and exquisite plants, it's a delightful place to stroll about and enjoy stunning views of the town and the shore.

The ancient brick and stone walls, an early jail, the officers' mess, many cannons, and a lighthouse are still standing.

Contextualizing the fort's history is the *Tobago Museum*, situated on the premises. It has collections of old maps, African art, shells, coins, and Native American artifacts.

Englishman's Bay, Tobago

Take a picnic basket to Englishman's Bay for a classic view of Tobago's coastline. It's worth the trip to this remote beach, which is 1.5 kilometers from Castara via a winding, narrow road. One of the best things to do in Tobago is to relax on these stunning coastlines.

Here stunning crescent of golden sand and jade-green water is tumbling down from hills covered in jungle and dotted with palm trees. If you're searching for the ideal picture to send home with your pals, here is the spot to grab your camera.

This charming stretch of beachfront is one of Trinidad & Tobago's most romantic spots because of its hidden position. The crystal-clear water is perfect for swimming and snorkeling, and if you want to enhance your beachside relaxation, the little café in the parking lot rents out chairs and umbrellas.

There are a few gift stores where you may purchase various trinkets and bamboo bird feeders. However, the landscape is the real star of the show.

Caroni Bird Sanctuary, Trinidad

For those who enjoy the outdoors, *Caroni Bird Sanctuary* (*Caroni Swamp*), located just south of Port of Spain, is a paradise. The national bird of Trinidad and Tobago, the scarlet ibis, nests throughout this network of mangrove-lined canals.

Boat trips in the afternoon look for these amazing flame-colored birds by cruising the estuaries. Take a trip just before dusk to get stunning pictures of the birds as they assemble in big groups to roost for the night on the trees. It's a fantastic image opportunity.

In addition to seeing a wide variety of other animal species, including herons, egrets, cormorants, tree boas, anteaters, and caimans, the region is rich in biodiversity. Tours for photography and fishing are also offered.

Little Tobago Island

One of the most significant seabird sanctuaries in the Caribbean is located on *Little Tobago Island*, which is located across from Speyside on the east end of the island. There are many kilometers of pathways winding through the dense vegetation on this isolated island.

For the most amazing views, look seaward from the hilltops where you may see vast groups of frigate birds, red-billed tropicbirds, and red-footed boobies swooping above. The island is home to around fifty different kinds of birds, including laughing gulls and Audubon's shearwater.

Tours: Glass-bottom boats glide you to the island and around the tiny *Goat Island* in *Tyrrell's Bay*, displaying the coral reefs underneath.

Hiking to the island's top and snorkeling on the adjacent reef are frequent additions to tours.

Mount St. Benedict Monastery, Trinidad

One of the most outstanding features east of Port of Spain is *Mount St. Benedict Monastery*, with its red-roofed church tower rising above the *Northern Range Hills* above Tunapuna.

This community was founded in 1912 by Benedictine monks, and the monastery is the oldest and biggest in the Caribbean. Including a farm, hotel, rehabilitation center, and religious structures, the monastery complex was established with the values of self-sufficiency and openness to outsiders.

The nearby forest offers plenty of hiking and birdwatching possibilities, and the monastery is well-known for its yogurt, which is sent to shops throughout the nation.

Pointe-a-Pierre Wildfowl Trust, Trinidad

Although visiting a wildlife refuge in the heart of an oil refinery may seem strange, this is one of Trinidad's prime locations for bird viewing.

Encircled by dense tropical vegetation, the 30-hectare sanctuary has an educational center and nature paths that meander across lakes crowned with lilies.

Here, you may observe species like the white-cheeked pintail, black-bellied whistling duck, and scarlet ibis.

Photographers seeking to get a close-up of one of these beautiful feathered creatures should definitely check out this location.

The Pointe-a-Pierre Wildfowl Trust manages captive breeding and rehabilitation initiatives for endangered birds in addition to safeguarding the sanctuary.

Main Ridge Forest Reserve, Tobago

The Main Ridge Forest Reserve, home to a wealth of wildlife, is said to be the oldest legally protected forest in the Western Hemisphere.

More than half of the island's bird species may be found in the reserve, including the uncommon white-tailed sabrewing hummingbird, collared trogon, and blue-backed manakin, among many other species.

As you hike among the thick vegetation, you may see butterflies, lizards, frogs, and snakes. One of the most scenic routes to see the forest is the road that runs through the reserve from north to south, close to Tobago's eastern tip.

There are hiking paths and independent guides to the top of the ridge.

Gasparee Caves

The Gasparee Caves, situated on *Gaspar Grande Island* in Trinidad and Tobago, provide a captivating insight into the hidden wonders of the Earth. These natural limestone caverns, shaped by millions of years of wave action and rain, showcase a wealth of geological formations, sparkling pools, and fascinating history.

Journey to Gaspar Grande:

Your adventure commences with a scenic boat trip from either *Chaguaramas* or *Port of Spain*, traversing the turquoise waters of the *Bocas del Dragon*. As you approach *Gaspar Grande*, an island adorned with mangroves, the anticipation builds for the undisclosed underground wonders it harbors.

Upon arrival, a brief hike through the island's lush rainforest leads to the entrance of the cave. Keep a lookout for diverse birdlife such as yellow-headed parrots and rufous-necked woodrails flitting through the foliage.

Entering the cool, dimly lit cave mouth, a sense of awe washes over you as towering rock formations, and glistening stalactites and stalagmites come into view. It is advisable to wear sturdy shoes due to the uneven and damp path.

Exploring the Captivating Blue Grotto:

The undisputed highlight of the *Gasparee Caves* is the *Blue Grotto*. This cavern features a mesmerizing crystal-clear pool, its aquamarine waters illuminated by dappled sunlight filtering through a collapsed portion of the cave ceiling.

While officially prohibited, certain guided tours with experienced guides may permit a brief dip in the refreshing waters of the *Blue Grotto*.

Imagine floating amidst the ethereal glow, surrounded by nature's artistry – an unforgettable experience.

As you navigate the chambers of the cave, marvel at the intriguing rock formations sculpted over time. Take note of imaginative names like "*The Buddha*," "*Virgin Mary*," and "*The Lovers*," inspiring your own interpretations of their shapes.

Planning Your Excursion:

To explore the *Gasparee Caves*, it is crucial to book a guided tour. These tours typically encompass the boat ride, hike, cave exploration, and insightful commentary from knowledgeable guides.

Remember to wear comfortable shoes, bring water and snacks, and be prepared for potentially slippery conditions.

Hanuman Statue

Towering above the village of *Carapichaima* in Trinidad and Tobago, *the Hanuman Statue* is a breathtaking spectacle. Soaring to a height of 85 feet, it not only stands as the most prominent landmark on the island but also holds the distinction of being the largest Hanuman murti (statue) outside of India, rendering it a significant symbol for both Trinidadian Hindus and Hindu devotees globally.

Lord Hanuman, venerated for his unwavering devotion *to Lord Rama,* incredible strength, and indomitable courage, epitomizes the ideal Hindu disciple. The statue impeccably captures his essence, portraying him with a resolute gaze, hands clasped in prayer, and a mace resting on his shoulder.

The temple complex encompassing the statue showcases elements of the intricate Dravidian style from South India, underscoring its ties to Hindu heritage. The vivid colors, elaborate carvings, and towering gopurams (gateways) contribute to its visual magnificence.

Situated on the grounds of the *Dattatreya Yoga Center and Mandir*, the statue serves as a centerpiece for this vibrant spiritual hub, offering yoga classes, meditation sessions, and religious ceremonies.

Visitors can immerse themselves in the serene atmosphere and seek blessings from the towering Hanuman.

Encountering the Hanuman Statue:

Accessible Areas: While the temple complex itself has restricted public access due to its active religious use, visitors can stroll around the *Hanuman Statue* and appreciate its grandeur from various perspectives.

Religious Reverence: It is important to dress modestly and respectfully when in the vicinity, recognizing it as a sacred space for many. Photography is allowed outside the temple, but consideration for ongoing religious ceremonies is paramount.

Planning Your Trip:

Location: The Hanuman Statue is situated at Datta Drive, Orangefield Road, in Carapichaima.

Operating Hours: While the temple's hours may vary, the surrounding grounds are generally open during daylight hours.

Guided Excursions: Consider participating in a guided tour to gain a deeper understanding of the statue's history, religious significance, and cultural context.

OUTDOOR ACTIVITIES

Here are some of the most popular outdoor activities you can experience in Trinidad and Tobago:

Nature Trails and Hiking:

Main Ridge Forest Reserve: Embark on a journey through the world's oldest rainforest, home to exotic flora and fauna like the Trinidad piping guan, the red-tailed boa, and the giant heliconia.

Hike to the summit of the Northern Range for panoramic views.

Yerette: Take in the verdant beauty of the Yerette hummingbird sanctuary, where over 16 species of these dazzling feathered jewels flit among the flowers. Follow the scenic trails and witness their mesmerizing aerial displays.

Waterfalls and Swimming:

Rio Seco Waterfall: Hike through the lush rainforest and discover the hidden gem of *Rio Seco Waterfall*. Take a refreshing dip in its crystal-clear pool, surrounded by the verdant foliage and cascading waters.

Maracas Bay: Relax on the golden sands of *Maracas Bay*, considered one of the most beautiful beaches in Trinidad. Enjoy the sun, swim in the turquoise waters, and enjoy the lively atmosphere with local vendors and beach bars.

Marine Adventures:

Scuba Diving and Snorkeling: Explore the vibrant underwater world of Tobago's *Buccoo Reef*, teeming with colorful coral formations, tropical fish, and marine turtles. Discover shipwrecks and hidden coves, or simply snorkel along the coral gardens for an underwater experience.

Kayaking and Stand-up Paddleboarding: Glide across the calm waters of the Caribbean Sea, paddling along the coastline or venturing into mangrove forests. Enjoy the serene beauty of the natural landscapes and spot playful dolphins or majestic manatees.

Other Thrilling Activities:

Birdwatching: With over 460 bird species recorded in Trinidad and Tobago, the islands are a paradise for birdwatchers.

Visit the Asa Wright Nature Centre or the Caroni Swamp for a chance to spot exotic species like the scarlet macaw, the hoatzin, and the Trinidad motmot

Ziplining and Canopy Tours: Embark on an adrenaline-pumping adventure through the rainforest canopy on a zipline tour. Soar through the treetops, enjoying scenic views and the thrill of the ride.

A PERFECT SEVEN-DAY ITINERARY FOR A TRIP TO TRINIDAD AND TOBAGO

Embrace the exotic blend of Caribbean charm and cultural delights with this 7-day itinerary for Trinidad and Tobago! From beautiful beaches to hidden rainforests, prepare to be captivated by the beauty and energy of these fascinating islands.

Day 1: Port of Spain and Ariapita Avenue

Morning: Immerse yourself in the bustling capital, *Port of Spain*. Explore *Queen's Park Savannah*, a sprawling urban oasis, and marvel at the Holy Trinity Cathedral's neo-Gothic architecture.

Afternoon: Indulge in Trinidadian cuisine with a lunch at *Roti Shop*, sampling delicious roti wraps filled with curried meats and vegetables.

Evening: Experience the city's vibrant nightlife on Ariapita Avenue. Enjoy live music and delicious street food at local pubs and restaurants.

Day 2: Maracas Bay and Asa Wright Nature Centre

Morning: Escape to the golden sands of *Maracas Bay*, a scenic paradise ideal for swimming, sunbathing, and soaking up the Caribbean vibes.

Afternoon: Travel to the lush *Asa Wright Nature Centre*, a haven for birdwatchers and nature enthusiasts. Hike through the rainforest trails, spot exotic birds like the hoatzin and the Trinidad motmot, and learn about the island's rich biodiversity.

Evening: Enjoy a traditional "Lime" (Trinidadian gathering) at the Centre, accompanied by local music and storytelling around a bonfire.

Day 3: Caroni Swamp and Gasparee Caves

Morning: Witness the breathtaking spectacle of thousands of scarlet ibis taking flight at sunset during a boat tour through the *Caroni Swamp*, a unique ecosystem teeming with wildlife.

Afternoon: Embark on an exciting adventure to the *Gasparee Caves,* hidden beneath the surface. Explore the chambers adorned with stalactites and stalagmites, and marvel at the *Blue Grotto*, a natural pool bathed in ethereal light.

Evening: Relish a delicious seafood dinner at a local restaurant in *Port of Spain*.

Day 4: Ferry to Tobago and Pigeon Point Beach

Morning: Take the scenic ferry ride from *Port of Spain* to *Scarborough*, Tobago.

Afternoon: Relax on the pristine sands of *Pigeon Point Beach*, fringed by coconut palms and lapped by turquoise waters. Enjoy watersports like kayaking and paddleboarding, or simply soak up the sun.

Evening: Savor a romantic beachfront dinner at a local restaurant under the starry sky.

Day 5: Buccoo Reef and Charlotteville Waterfall

Morning: Dive into the underwater world of *Buccoo Reef*, a vibrant coral reef teeming with colorful fish, turtles, and marine life. Snorkel or scuba dive amongst the breathtaking coral formations.

Afternoon: Hike through the lush rainforest to reach the refreshing *Charlotteville Waterfall*, a hidden gem perfect for a swim in the cool waters surrounded by the verdant landscape.

Evening: Immerse yourself in the lively atmosphere of *Charlotteville village*, enjoying local music and sampling street food at the Friday night market.

Day 6: Little Tobago Island and Speyside

Morning: Take a boat tour to explore the uninhabited gem of *Little Tobago Island*. Hike through the rainforest, spot exotic birds like the red-footed booby, and snorkel in the crystal-clear waters.

Afternoon: Travel to the charming fishing village of *Speyside*, known for its beautiful beaches and relaxed atmosphere. Swim, sunbathe, or try your hand at surfing or kitesurfing.

Evening: Enjoy a delicious fresh seafood dinner at a local restaurant overlooking the sunset.

Day 7: Relax and Depart

Morning: Spend your last day soaking up the sun on the beach, reminiscing about your adventures, and indulging in final moments of Caribbean bliss.

Afternoon: Bid farewell to Tobago and take the ferry back to *Port of Spain* for your departure.

Tip:

During your trip, keep an eye out for traditional Carnival celebrations, a vibrant explosion of music, costumes, and dancing that takes place annually.

BEST BEACHES IN
TRINIDAD AND TOBAGO

Blessed with captivating beaches renowned for their tranquil waters and soft sands, Trinidad and Tobago offer a diverse range of experiences for every visitor.

Whether you seek an idyllic spot for snorkeling and encountering underwater wildlife or a coastline steeped in pirate history, these shores cater to various preferences. Each beach possesses its own unique charm, making Trinidad and Tobago the quintessence of sun, sea, and sand.

Maracas Bay, Trinidad:

Situated on Trinidad's north coast, *Maracas Bay* is the island's most popular beach, accessible via a winding mountain road.

Breathtaking scenery unfolds with palm trees, golden sands, and enveloping green mountains against the backdrop of wavy waters.

Beach vendors offer local treats, including the must-try deep-fried shark sandwich with spicy sauce, a popular choice among visitors.

Tyrico Beach, Trinidad:

For those seeking a quieter alternative to Maracas, *Tyrico Beach*, located at the eastern end of the same bay, provides a serene escape without the bustling facilities. The calmer waters here are perfect for paddling and enjoying a more relaxed beach experience.

Las Cuevas Bay, Trinidad:

Named for the numerous caves along its 2km stretch, *Las Cuevas* is the only Blue Flag certified beach in Trinidad and Tobago. The calm and clear waters make it ideal for swimming, with well-thought-out facilities and lifeguard services available. The western end offers opportunities for surfing during the winter months.

Blanchisseuse Beach, Trinidad:

Nestled on the north coast, *Blanchisseuse Beach* is a natural beauty bordered by rainforest, palms, and sea grapes. The golden sands, surfy sea, and rocky outcrops create a perfect setting.

Visitors can paddle in the river that flows into the sea and may witness leatherback turtles laying their eggs between March and August.

Macqueripe Beach, Trinidad:

Located at the far end of *Tucker Valley Road* on the *Chaguaramas peninsula, Macqueripe Beach* is a smaller bay surrounded by hilly tropical forest.

With clear waters and opportunities for swimming, snorkeling, and a thrilling zip line nearby, it offers a tranquil escape.

Mayaro Beach, Trinidad:

On the southwest coast, *Mayaro Beach* boasts golden sands that form Trinidad's longest beach. Ideal for beach walks and kayaking, it offers a serene atmosphere. Lifeguards are present to guide visitors to safe swimming spots due to undercurrents in certain areas.

Pigeon Point Beach, Tobago:

Situated at the tip of *Pigeon Point Heritage Park*, this beach on the south end of Tobago is known for its white sand, palms, and turquoise sea.

Divided into Main Beach, North Beach, and South Beach, each section has its unique character, providing a classic Caribbean experience.

Englishman's Bay Beach, Tobago:

Despite being one of Tobago's most beautiful beaches, *Englishman's Bay* maintains a peaceful atmosphere. Backed by rainforest, it features golden sand, almond trees, and clear waters in varying shades of blue.

Activities include swimming, snorkeling, and sunbathing, with Eula's restaurant offering tasty roti, fresh fish, and handcrafted gifts.

Pirate's Bay Beach, Tobago:

Accessible via a rickety road and steps or by boat from *Charlotteville, Pirate's Bay Beach* offers pale yellow sands, blue-green waters, and emerald trees.

Once a refuge for pirates, this isolated beach provides a dreamlike setting for swimming, snorkeling, and solitude, although it lacks facilities.

Buccoo Bay, Tobago:

Buccoo Bay boasts a mile of white sand and turquoise waters, sheltered by the stunning *Buccoo Reef*, one of the world's most spectacular marine parks. Snorkelers will find the marine life fascinating.

On Sunday evenings, visitors can join the Sunday School Street party featuring local musicians, street food, and dancing.

DINING IN TRINIDAD AND TOBAGO

Local Dishes and Specialties

The twin-island nation is renowned for its various culinary heritage, influenced by a myriad of cultures. Throughout history, both colonizers and enslaved populations have significantly shaped the islands' food culture, resulting in a rare and exceptional diversity within the cuisine of the Republic of Trinidad and Tobago, setting it apart in the Caribbean.

The most beloved dishes derive from various countries, including India, Africa, Syria, and Spain. The culinary influences are evident in dishes such as Indian curry, Spanish-inspired Pastelles, and African dasheen.

However, it is the fusion of these influences and distinct flavors that gives rise to the popularity of the remaining dishes. These delectable offerings are readily accessible, particularly on the island of Trinidad.

Below are some must-try foods that will surely whet your appetite during a visit to these islands.

Street Food

Doubles:

Undoubtedly the most popular street food on the island, Doubles resembles a vegetarian sandwich. It consists of two *baras* (pieces of fried dough) filled with *channa* (chickpea) and topped with various sauces, including pepper sauce, cilantro sauce, tamarind sauce, coconut chutney, grated cucumber, or kuchela, often combining all of the above.

Aloo Pie:

Aloo pie is a deep-fried pocket filled with spiced mashed potatoes (aloo is the Hindi word for potato). The potatoes are cooked with *chadon-beni* and garlic. The fried dough is sliced open, filled with curried chickpeas, sprinkled with pepper and/or tamarind sauce, and adorned with various other toppings.

Saheena:

Saheena is a mouthwatering and beloved street food, especially popular during *Divali* (the Hindu festival of lights). The soul of this dish lies in the vibrant emerald of dasheen leaves, the warmth of turmeric, and the complex dance of fragrant spices, all bound together by the earthy nuttiness of yellow split pea flour.

Pholourie:

Another favorite street food, *Pholourie*, consists of fried blobs made from a batter of chickpea flour seasoned with garlic, onion, turmeric, and peppers, then deep-fried. Typically, they are served with tamarind or mango chutney.

Chow:

Fruits are abundant on the island of Trinidad, and chow is a spicy preparation of chopped fruit, usually mango or pineapple, marinated in lime juice, black pepper, garlic, and chadon-beni.

Bake and Shark:

Bake and shark feature two pieces of fried dough filled with a fried fillet of shark. The toppings are customizable and may include mustard, ketchup, pepper sauce, sliced cucumber, pineapple, tomatoes, lettuce, mayonnaise, or *chadon-beni* sauce. This dish is commonly found on the beach.

Gyro:

Trinidadian Gyro, influenced by the Syrian/Lebanese population, features spit-roasted meat with local vegetables and sauces, creating a unique twist on this favorite meal.

Souse:

Made from either chicken feet or pig's trotters, Souse involves marinating cucumbers in lime juice, onion, and peppers. While its appearance may not be initially appealing, adventurous foodies find it to be a snack worth trying.

Barbecued Pigtail:

Reflecting the island's tradition of minimizing waste, Barbecued Pigtail transforms cheap cuts into delicious meals.

Black Pudding:

Despite its misleading name, Black Pudding is a sausage made with pig's blood, local herbs, and various spices. It is often enjoyed with local bread called hops or by itself with pepper sauce, showcasing an acquired taste.

Meat Dishes

Crab and Dumpling:

This dish consists of sticky pieces of unevenly cut dumplings cooked in a mild coconut-milk curry sauce with crab.

Despite being a messy meal, its deliciousness makes it worth indulging in. Crab and Dumpling is predominantly found on the island of Tobago.

Pelau:

Pelau is a one-pot dish featuring stewed meat cooked with rice and vegetables. The meat is first marinated in seasoning and then caramelized in oil and sugar.

After caramelization, rice, vegetables, and coconut milk are added to the pot to complete the dish.

Oil Down:

In Oil Down, vegetables are stewed in coconut milk until absorbed, leaving a small amount of coconut oil at the bottom of the pan, hence its name. Breadfruit is commonly used in the preparation of this flavorful meal.

Pastelles:

Traditionally made during the Christmas season, *Pastelles* have roots tracing back to the Spanish colonizers. These cornmeal-based delights are stuffed with beef, pork, chicken, or a combination of these meats. The final touch involves wrapping them in banana leaves and steaming.

Roti:

Roti comes in various variations, with the most common types in Trinidad and Tobago being paratha and dhalpuri. Paratha has a soft and flaky texture, while Dhal Puri is filled with split peas.

Both types are typically served with either vegetables or curried meats, and regardless of the choice, eating with hands is customary.

Vegetarian Food

Buljol:

To prepare *Buljol*, salted fish pieces are soaked and boiled, then flaked and mixed with hot peppers, sweet peppers, onions, tomatoes, garlic, and oil.

This savory dish is commonly enjoyed for breakfast and is typically paired with hops or fried bake.

Coo-Coo:

Coo-coo is a straightforward meal crafted from cornmeal and okra.

Callaloo:

Callaloo, with its roots in West Africa, is a one-pot wonder resembling a soup. It is often served with rice, macaroni pie, and stewed chicken for Sunday lunch.

In Trinidad and Tobago, this dish features dasheen plant leaves and stems cooked down with pumpkin, okra, onions, spices, peppers, and coconut milk to create a creamy and flavorful dish.

Dhal:

Reflecting the strong Indian influence in Trinidad and Tobago, there is a Trinbagonian style of *Dhal*. This dish requires time for preparation and cooking, involving boiling split peas until they soften or soaking them overnight.

Prepared with ingredients such as garlic, onions, pepper, and turmeric or saffron, Dhal is commonly served with rice.

Soups

Cowheel Soup:

The tradition of soup consumption in the islands has deep historical roots dating back to the days of slavery and indentured labor.

Soups remain a popular dish in the country, particularly on Saturdays. Cowheel soup is a flavorful concoction made with peas and beef.

Fish Broth:

A delectable soup, fish broth features a blend of vegetables, fresh herbs, fish, noodles, and dumplings. The flavor of the broth is largely influenced by the seasoning of the fish.

Corn Soup:

This hearty soup is brimming with corn, potatoes, carrots, yellow split peas, pumpkin, dumplings, and various spices, all immersed in a rich coconut-based broth. Often served as a post-event meal on the streets after football games and late-night parties, this soup has become a ubiquitous choice for many.

Desserts and Sweets

Pone:

For a delightful dessert experience, be sure to try the cassava pone of Trinidad and Tobago. This mouthwatering treat is primarily composed of grated cassava, coconut, and pumpkin.

Bound together with a blend of sugar, cinnamon, milk, and raisins, it possesses a thick, sticky, and moist texture.

Kurma:

A well-loved Indian sweet, *Kurma* is traditionally prepared during Divali (a Hindu Festival) and is also served at Hindu weddings.

This delectable treat features fried ginger-spiced dough coated in sugar syrup, left to harden for a delightful crunch.

Soursop Ice Cream:

A particularly popular dessert in Trinidad and Tobago, *Soursop Ice Cream* is crafted from ripe soursop, water, cornstarch, condensed milk, salt, and a touch of bitters.

This delightful ice cream offers a unique and refreshing flavor.

Best Places to Eat

Tree Top Restaurant, situated in Speyside, Tobago, is renowned for its picturesque beachfront location and delectable seafood offerings. The standout dish is the lobster in garlic sauce, complemented by a diverse menu featuring Creole and Caribbean cuisine.

Lola's Food Company, located in *Port of Spain*, offers a contemporary twist on Trinidadian cuisine. The menu boasts a wide array of dishes, such as chicken and waffles, saltfish omelette, and black angus footlong hotdogs.

Additionally, they present a popular Christmas menu featuring ham sandwiches, waffles, and pancakes.

Shiann's Food Palace, also situated in Port of Spain, is celebrated for its blend of Indian and Trinidadian flavors. The menu features a diverse selection of dishes, including rice, dhal, roti, curry, seafood specialties, pasta dishes, and sandwiches.

The Meena House, an upscale restaurant located in *Chaguanas*, offers a fusion of Indian and international cuisine in an elegant setting. Signature dishes include tandoori lobster, lamb Rogan Josh, and butter chicken.

Samurai Restaurant, situated in *Cascade*, is a lively establishment specializing in fresh sushi, sashimi, and Japanese delicacies. The Samurai Roll, featuring tempura shrimp, crab, and avocado, is a highlight.

Salus Lifestyle, a health-conscious cafe in St. Augustine, provides a variety of vegetarian, vegan, and gluten-free options. Their menu includes quinoa bowls, lentil burgers, and coconut water smoothies.

Edge of the Reef, perched on a cliff in *Speyside*, Tobago, offers breathtaking views of the Caribbean Sea. Specializing in fresh seafood, the menu includes grilled lobster, blackened fish, and conch fritters.

Tobago Paradise Travel and Grill, located in Crown Point, Tobago, is a beachside restaurant offering a laid-back atmosphere and delicious Caribbean fare. The menu features items like jerk chicken, coconut shrimp, and flying fish sandwiches.

Caribbean Kitchen at Castara Retreats, nestled in *Castara Bay*, Tobago, provides a taste of the islands with flavorful Caribbean, Cajun, and Creole dishes. Menu highlights include Trinidad callaloo soup, roti with stewed chicken, and blackened shrimp Creole.

Richard's Bake & Shark, situated in Maracas Bay, is an iconic shack serving up the quintessential Trinidadian street food: bake and shark, a must-try for any visitor to Trinidad.

SHOPPING IN TRINIDAD AND TOBAGO

Best Local Markets

Trinidad and Tobago is renowned for its lively local markets that provide an immersive experience of sights, scents, and flavors. These markets serve as cultural hubs, allowing visitors to interact with locals, haggle for souvenirs, and indulge in some of the most delicious street food imaginable. Here's a rundown of some outstanding local markets in Trinidad and Tobago, each possessing its distinctive allure:

Tunapuna Market:

Situated in *Tunapuna*, a lively town to the east of *Port of Spain*, *Tunapuna Market* is a veritable trove of fresh produce, spices, and indigenous crafts.

Visitors can explore stalls brimming with exotic fruits such as passionfruit, soursop, and guavas, alongside an array of vegetables, herbs, and spices that promise a tantalizing culinary experience.

Ensure you partake in local street delights, such as pholourie (deep-fried chickpea balls) and roti (flatbread filled with curried potatoes or meat).

Open daily from sunrise to sunset, Tunapuna Market offers a genuine glimpse into Trinidadian life.

Ariapita Market:

Discover the street culture of *Ariapita Market*, situated in the *Woodbrook* neighborhood of Port of Spain.

This market is a lively display of colors and sounds, with vendors peddling a variety of items, from clothing and jewelry to handmade crafts and household goods.

Don't miss the chance to sample some of the local delicacies, like bake and shark (deep-fried shark served on fried dough) and coocoo (cornmeal and okra soup).

Open on Fridays and Saturdays, *Ariapita Market* is a must-visit for those seeking an authentic Trinidadian experience.

Maco Market:

Head to Tobago's crown jewel, *Scarborough*, and explore the bustling Maco Market.

This market is a kaleidoscope of local fruits and vegetables, fresh seafood, and traditional Tobagonian crafts.

Don't forget to acquire some of the island's renowned nutmeg and cinnamon, ideal for bringing home as a memento.

Open daily, *Maco Market* provides an excellent opportunity to stock up on groceries and engage with the amiable locals.

Charlotteville Market:

Nestled in the beautiful village of *Charlotteville* on Tobago's north coast, this market offers a taste of island life.

Expect to encounter fresh fish caught that morning, locally grown fruits and vegetables, and handcrafted souvenirs made by skilled artisans.

Enjoy local specialties like crab and callaloo soup or stewed chicken with dumplings.

Open on weekdays, *Charlotteville Market* is a charming locale to experience the unhurried pace of life in Tobago.

St. James Market:

For a unique market experience, venture to *St. James Market* in *Port of Spain*.

This market hosts a wide range of vendors selling antiques, collectibles, artwork, and clothing.

You're certain to discover something distinctive and memorable to bring back as a keepsake.

Open on Fridays and Saturdays, *St. James Market* is an excellent place to explore and uncover hidden treasures.

Local Products and Souvenirs to Buy

When shopping in Trinidad & Tobago, take into account the following regional goods and mementos:

Steelpan Instruments:

The steelpan, an instrument constructed of oil drums, originated in Trinidad and Tobago. As mementos, visitors may purchase small steelpan reproductions or even real, handmade instruments.

Regional Handicrafts and Art:

Skilled regional artists produce vivid paintings, sculptures, and crafts that reflect the island's culture and scenery. Seek for distinctive works that encapsulate the spirit of the creative community in Trinidad & Tobago.

Handmade Bags and Baskets:

Handwoven baskets and bags, made from natural materials like straw and reeds, are a testament to the islands' traditional artistry. These things are not only useful, but they also provide fashionable and environmentally responsible keepsakes.

Textiles using Batik and Tie-Dye:

The vibrant batik and tie-dye textiles of Trinidad and Tobago are well-known worldwide. These eye-catching and distinctively designed articles of clothes, scarves, and even fabric are available for purchase by the yard.

Seasonings and Spices:

The spices and seasonings found on the islands give Trinidadian and Tobagonian food a unique taste. Curry blends, spice mixtures, and spicy pepper sauces made locally are popular options.

Cocoa & Products Made with Chocolate:

Trinidad and Tobago are known for their high-quality cocoa beans. Chocolate bars, cocoa tea, and even cosmetic goods made with cocoa are available for purchase by tourists. Seek for goods from nearby cocoa fields and chocolatiers.

Angostura Bitters:

Angostura Bitters, a well-known fragrant bitters used in cocktails all over the globe, is made in Trinidad and Tobago. In addition to other goods from the Angostura firm, like flavored rums and rum, visitors may purchase bottles of Angostura Bitters.

Local Spirits and Rum:

The rum business in Trinidad and Tobago is doing quite well. Tourists may buy bottles of aged rum or flavored spirits and tour the local distillery. Reputable companies like Angostura and Caroni are great gift options for their merchandise.

Caribbean Fashion and Clothing:

The fashion industry in Trinidad and Tobago is thriving, with designers producing chic apparel that draws inspiration from the region's culture. Look for gowns, beachwear, and accessories that are made in the area.

Customized Jewelry:

Local jewelers create one-of-a-kind items that are influenced by the islands' scenic splendor. Seek for jewelry that captures the tropical appeal of the Caribbean using native materials, seashells, and jewels found in the area.

NIGHTLIFE IN TRINIDAD AND TOBAGO

Best Bars and Nightclubs

Port of Spain

Club Zen: For fans of electronic music, this chic *Woodbrook* nightclub is a sanctuary. *Club Zen* promises an amazing night with cutting edge sound systems, eye-catching light displays, and international DJs performing the newest music.

Jade Monkey Casino & Bar: Are you itching for a glamorous evening at *Jade Monkey Casino & Bar?* Jade Monkey is the only place to look. This elegant casino bar on *Ariapita Avenue* combines live music, a classy atmosphere, and high-stakes gambling. Enjoy their delectable sushi plates and specialty beverages.

D'Lime Bar & Restaurant: Both residents and visitors love this vibrant location in *St. Clair*. At D'Lime, you can enjoy a laid-back evening of cocktails and conversation with a cuisine brimming with Caribbean flavors, a big outdoor terrace, and friendly bartenders.

Situated in *Woodbrook*, **Smokey & Bunty** has a cozy and welcoming ambiance. Catch up with friends and enjoy a laid-back night out at *Smokey & Bunty*, which offers substantial pub meals, a large range of drinks, and live music on weekends.

Ariapita Avenue:

The Foundry is a hip gastropub in *Woodbrook* that combines delicious food with an industrial aesthetic. With its creative tapas-style cuisine, broad beverage menu, and live music, The Foundry offers a savory and lively experience.

The Yacht Club: Sail away on an experience with a nautical atmosphere at *The Yacht Club*. Renowned for its lively environment, courteous service, and rum drinks, this pub is located on *Ariapita Avenue*. Drink a "Painkiller" while you take in the Caribbean atmosphere and sway to reggae music.

Tobago

Situated directly on Store Bay Beach, **Coconut Beach Bar & Grill** is the quintessential island getaway. As the sun sets, enjoy fresh seafood, sip tropical beverages, and dance to Soca music.

Partygoers are drawn to Crown Point's vibrant nightclub, **Blue Iguana.** A night of unrestrained dancing and celebration is guaranteed at *Blue Iguana* with its throbbing Soca tunes, exuberant DJs, and lively audience.

Tucked away in Speyside, **Moriah Bar & Seafood Restaurant** is a hidden treasure that serves delicious seafood meals, a laid-back environment, and breathtaking coastal views. Savor a romantic meal al fresco while taking in the calming sound of the waves lapping against the coast.

BEST PLACES TO STAY

The Port of Spain is the ideal location for lodging in Trinidad and Tobago. The well-known Carnival and other exciting activities may be found in the capital city!

However, as you may be aware, this nation is really made up of two islands, so there are many more interesting places, such as *Grande Riviere, Scarborough, Crown Point,* and *Black Rock,* that are ideal for a variety of hobbies and families as well as nature lovers and those seeking a fully-rounded experience.

We'll discuss each location and let you know where to discover the greatest lodging options and entertaining activities!

PORT OF SPAIN – BEST PLACE TO STAY FOR FIRST TIMERS

The capital city of Port of Spain is the best spot to rent a hotel if you're visiting the stunning islands of Trinidad and Tobago for the first time. Book your rent well in advance, however, since this Caribbean island is becoming more popular with travelers!

This region of Trinidad and Tobago is ideal for travelers looking for a well-rounded experience since it is home to the island's well-known event, the Carnival, as well as several historical sites.

You'll get lost for hours exploring all the activities and taking in the stunning architecture! By the way, I suggest expanding your list of things to do in Trinidad and Tobago to include visiting the *National Museum & Art Gallery, Queen's Park Savannah,* and the *Botanical Gardens.*

Port of Spain, which is also well-known for its exciting nightlife and long range of dining options, will undoubtedly win your heart!

Hotels in Port of Spain

Hyatt Regency Trinidad

The Hyatt Regency Trinidad has an outdoor infinity pool, a state-of-the-art gym, and a business center. It is five minutes' walk from the Ferry Terminal and Trinidad and Tobago Water Taxi.

The air-conditioned rooms include a private bathroom, a flat-screen cable TV, and iPod docks. Some apartments feature views of the sea or a balcony.

In addition, the Hyatt Regency provides 9,000 square feet of space for a spa and fitness center, a lobby bar and lounge, and a full-service waterfront restaurant. Business travelers may unwind in style at the Hyatt Regency Trinidad, which has an infinity pool, a poolside restaurant, and a terrace with views of the *Gulf of Paria*.

Located in the Port of Spain International Waterfront Development, Hyatt Regency Trinidad was intended as a Caribbean conference, convention, business, event, and leisure travel facility. In addition, the hotel has meeting spaces, valet parking, and laundry facilities.

Piarco International Airport is 30 minutes' drive away, while Maraca Bay Beach is 45 minutes' drive away.

Hotel Kapok

The Kapok Hotel is five minutes' walk from *Ellerslie Plaza* and *Queen's Park Savannah*. It has a sun patio, lawn, and swimming pool. There's free WiFi all around.

Air conditioning, a couch, a resting space, and a flat-screen cable TV are included in the rooms. There is a refrigerator and coffee machine in every room. The flat has a fully functional kitchen as well.

The on-site restaurants of the Kapok Hotel provide breakfast, lunch, and supper. The lobby also has a store.

A short stroll will take you to a variety of stores, eateries, and tourist sites. The city center, which includes Independence Square and Woodford Square, is five minutes away by car. It is 25 kilometers to Piarco International Airport.

Trinidad Gingerbread House

An inexpensive hotel with sun deck, coffee makers, and cozy rooms overlooking the garden. There is a terrace with a garden view in every room.

There is a fridge in each guest room.

The distance between Trinidad Gingerbread House and Las Cuevas is 20 km and 14 km, respectively.

GRANDE RIVIERE – BEST AREA FOR NATURE LOVERS

I am aware that a lot of you would rather be in a more serene setting with only the enormous ocean and some vegetation around you! If this's what you're searching for, Grande Riviere, on the island's north shore, is ideal.

Hiking trips to waterfalls, bird-watching excursions, and turtle-watching expeditions are all well-known in this secluded, environmentally friendly location! It is such a delight to be here as a nature lover!

Since the island's northeast shore serves as a major leatherback turtle breeding area, the whole region is really worth investigating!

Hotels in Grand Riviere

Hotel Acajou

Nestled in *Grande Riviere Bay* between the beach, the river, and the mountains is an environmentally conscious hotel. Free private parking, trips for viewing birds and turtles, and free Wi-Fi are all included.

The Acajou Hotel's cottages provide views of the river, a fan, a mosquito net, and tropical décor. Each private bathroom is equipped with its own shower.

The on-site restaurant serves a fusion of Swedish and Trinitarian food, while the Acajou's menu also includes continental and local dishes prepared with organic ingredients from the nearby farms or garden.

For an additional fee, the Acajou Hotel may set up shuttle services, boat trips, and airport transportation. During the season, visitors may take pleasure in seeing hatchling turtles make their way from the beach to the ocean.

This property is located one hour's boat ride from *Paria Falls* and five minutes' walk from the bird watching location. Driving time to *Piarco International Airport* is two hours and thirty minutes.

Le Grand Almandier

You can anticipate a bar, laundry facilities, and a complimentary full breakfast at *Le Grand Almandier*. Give yourself a massage or any other spa treatments. Local food is served *at Le Chateau Almandier,* the on-site restaurant. Free in-room WiFi allows you to stay connected.

While there, you'll also benefit from the following advantages:

Free on-site parking

One conference room, a front desk safe, and an airport shuttle (fee)

Features of the Rooms

At *Le Grand Almandier*, every guestroom has air conditioning, a furnished balcony, free WiFi, and safes, among other thoughtful details.

Additional amenities in every accommodation consist of:

Free cribs and baby beds, as well as rollaway/extra beds (surcharge)

Shower rooms and complimentary toiletries

22-inch plasma displays with satellite programming.

SCARBOROUGH – WHERE TO STAY FOR A WHOLESOME EXPERIENCE

Even while you like the city, you still wish the beach was close by? No worries, this amazing location on the island of Tobago provides the ideal blend!

City living with a hint of sandy beaches and azure oceans!

Scarborough, which lies on the western side of the island, is also the location of Tobago's major port and a plethora of eateries and pubs! Yes, nothing compares to strolling through the crowded streets of the island late at night.

Hotels in Scarborough

Faith's Villa of Tobago

These apartments in Diamond, Tobago, are just 800 meters from *Little Rockly Bay*. They provide views of the ocean, bright, tasteful décor, and free Wi-Fi.

Every unit at Faith's Villa of Tobago has a dining and sitting room in addition to a fully functional kitchen. They have cable TV and complete air conditioning.

If visitors would want to prepare meals at home, there is a small grocery 3 kilometers away from the property, and restaurants offering both domestic and foreign cuisine can be found in Scarborough, the next town, 5 minutes away by vehicle.

Faith's Villa of Tobago is located ten minutes' drive from the well-known *Mount Irvin Beach*, and visitors may reach a retail center in five minutes.

Comfort Inn & Suites Tobago

In Tobago, Comfort Inn & Suites has a garden, a fitness center, an outdoor pool, and a common lounge. This 3-star hotel has free WiFi, free shuttle service, and free room service. Free private parking is offered, and there's an American restaurant on site.

Every apartment has complimentary amenities, a desk, a refrigerator, a microwave, a coffee maker, air conditioning, and a bath or shower. A hairdryer, bed linens, and a private bathroom are included in every guest room.

The Tobago Comfort Inn & Suites has a patio.

The lodging has on-site vending machines with food and beverages as well as a business center. At the front desk, employees speak both Spanish and English.

Cocoa Cabana

Cocoa Cabana is a newly remodeled guest home with a garden in Scarborough. The home has views of the garden and the river. Guests may check in and out privately, and there's a common kitchen at the lodging.

To ensure that visitors have a quiet stay, the guest house apartments include soundproofing and individual entrances. Free WiFi is available in all of the guest house's accommodations, which also include private bathrooms with showers and some rooms with terraces. Each guest room at the guest home has towels and bed linens.

There is a picnic area at the guest house where you may enjoy a day outside.

CROWN POINT – BEST PLACE TO STAY FOR BEACH GOERS

The stunning beaches of the Caribbean are well-known! Therefore, seek for hotels here if you want to spend the most of your time exploring Tobago's sandy coastlines.

For those who want to stay close to Tobago's international airport, Crown Point is an excellent choice. This region, which is in southwest Tobago, is ideal for anybody who wants the necessities to be close at hand. It is really rather developed in terms of dining options, drinking establishments, and lodging.

This side of the island has a lot of lovely beaches like *Store Bay Beach*, and even some close by. It takes around 30 minutes to walk to *Pigeon Point Beach*, which is well-known for its scenic vistas. You won't even be able to sense the distance if you just stroll down the shore!

Hotels in Crown Point

Nest Villa

The Nest Villa, A Dream Escape for the whole family is located in *Golden Grove*, Tobago, and offers accommodations with free WiFi and free private parking.

The villa has a living room, five bathrooms, and five separate bedrooms. The lodging does not allow smoking.

Nzingha's Villa

Nzingha's Villa is located in Buccoo and offers free WiFi and accommodations with a rooftop pool. This lodging offers views of the inner courtyard and a terrace. The property is located 1.3 kilometers from Buccoo Beach and is non-smoking.

The large villa has a dining area, a fully supplied kitchen, a balcony with views of the pool, three bedrooms, two bathrooms, towels, bed linens, and a flat-screen TV with satellite channels.

In addition, there is a sitting space and two bathrooms with walk-in showers in the air-conditioned villa. The lodging has a separate entrance and round-the-clock security for more privacy.

The villa offers a car-rental service.

Nzingha's Villa is located 1.8 kilometers from *Mount Irvine Bay Beach*.

Carolina Point Resort

Carolina Point Resort is a BBQ and sun terrace resort near Crown Point, Tobago Region. Complimentary private parking is available on the premises at no cost.

A cable flat-screen TV and air conditioning are features shared by all apartments. Certain apartments provide a patio or eating space. There's also a coffee maker and microwave.

Some of the apartments include kitchens as well, complete with a refrigerator, oven, and toaster. Free WiFi is available throughout Carolina Point Resort. There is bed linen available.

Water activities are prominent in the region, and the hotel offers bike rentals.

Diving and snorkeling are among the activities that visitors may partake in nearby. Less than a kilometer away from the resort is Tobago Airport, the closest airport.

BLACK ROCK: A FAMILY'S BEST PLACE TO STAY IN TOBAGO

I would suggest lodging at Black Rock if you're traveling with little children since this region has a ton of watersports that are guaranteed to please everyone!

You're probably wondering why it's named "*Black Rock*" at this point.

As you can see, there are black rocks all around the beaches here. In fact, there are rumors that the beach is situated on a large black rock!

Your children may find that entertaining!

As I said, you may try your hand at swimming, snorkeling, surfing, and other water sports while you're here! You may visit a number of restaurants and other cultural sites here as well.

Hotels in Black Rock

Plantation Beach Villas

Facing *Stonehaven Bay*, Plantation Beach Villa provides free private parking, WiFi, terraces, gardens, and an outdoor pool for its visitors.

The villa has a dining area, a patio, a private bathroom with a shower, and an equipped kitchen. The property also has a safety deposit box and bedrooms with air conditioning. The decor follows a plantation style theme.

Although the fully furnished kitchens of Plantation Beach Villas allow guests to prepare meals on their own, the villa also provides culinary services. In addition, there is a bar on the premises, and massage services are extra-charged.

In addition, Plantation Beach Villa has table tennis, volleyball, kayaking, and massages on your balcony. Our office can also set you up for sailing, scuba diving, rain forest and tour trips, sports fishing, and even a glass-bottom boat ride on Buccoo Reef.

Studio One

Studio One is 1.6 kilometers from *Plymouth Beach* and 1 km from *Mount Irvine Bay Beach* in Black Rock. It has air conditioning and a yard. There is free WiFi, free private parking, and a private pool on this property.

The apartment has one bedroom, one bathroom, towels, bed linens, a fully functional kitchen, a flat-screen TV with streaming services, and a balcony with views of the garden.

BEST TRAVEL RESOURCES

These are the best travel resources I usually use:

SkyScanner: This is my favorite flight search engine of all time. It always appears to discover the greatest rates, and its calendar display shows you when days are the most affordable to travel. It appeals to me since it searches little booking sites that no one else does. Begin all of your flight searches here.

Momodo: This fantastic website searches a wide range of airlines, including several low-cost carriers that bigger sites overlook. While I usually start with Skyscanner, I'll also look at this site to compare costs.

Google Flights: Google Flights allows you to input your departure airport and view flights all around the globe on a map to get the cheapest destination. It's a useful search engine for learning about routes, connections, and prices.

Hostelworld: The market's most user-friendly hostel website, with the greatest inventory, the finest search interface, and the most availability. You may also look for private rooms or dorm beds. I use it for my reservations.

Couchsurfing: This website enables you to stay for free on people's sofas or in their spare rooms. It's a terrific way to save money while meeting locals who can teach you a lot more about a place than a hostel or hotel can. There are also groups on the web where you can organize to meet up for activities in your location.

Booking.com: Booking.com is an excellent resource for low-cost hotels and other forms of lodging. I enjoy how simple its UI is.

Trusted Housesitters: Try house- or pet-sitting for a novel (and free) way to travel. You just care after someone's home and/or pet while they are gone in return for free lodging. It's an excellent choice for long-term travelers and those on a tight budget.

CONCLUSION

In the heart of the Caribbean, where the rhythm of life matches the beat of the steelpan and the warmth of the sun mirrors the hospitality of its people, lies the enchanting duo of Trinidad and Tobago. As we conclude this travel guide, the vibrant tapestry of these islands beckons travelers to immerse themselves in an unforgettable tapestry of culture, nature, and adventure.

Trinidad, the bustling larger sibling, pulsates with energy. From the lively markets of Port of Spain to the rhythmic sounds of Carnival, this island is a celebration of diversity. Exploring the Tunapuna Market becomes a sensory journey, with stalls overflowing with exotic fruits and spices, encapsulating the essence of Trinidadian cuisine. The infectious rhythm of the steelpan resonates through the streets, a testament to the island's musical prowess and the birthplace of this unique instrument.

Venturing into the Woodbrook neighborhood, the Ariapita Market invites visitors to revel in the kaleidoscope of colors and sounds, where local vendors showcase their craftsmanship in handmade crafts and jewelry. The delectable aromas of bake and shark and coocoo lure you into a culinary exploration, revealing the rich flavors that define Trinidad's street food scene.

In Scarborough, Tobago's crown jewel, the Maco Market emerges as a vibrant kaleidoscope of local produce, seafood, and traditional crafts. Here, the bounty of the land and sea converges, offering a glimpse into the island's culinary and artisanal heritage. Nutmeg and cinnamon, indigenous treasures, find their way into the market stalls, inviting visitors to take home a piece of Tobago's aromatic charm.

Journeying to the picturesque village of Charlotteville on Tobago's north coast, the Charlotteville Market embodies the serene rhythm of island life. Freshly caught fish, locally grown fruits, and the artistry of skilled artisans converge in a delightful showcase of Tobagonian culture. The market becomes a haven for those seeking a respite from the hustle, inviting them to savor the flavors of crab and callaloo soup or stewed chicken with dumplings.

For those with a penchant for the unique, the St. James Market in Port of Spain stands as a treasure trove of hidden gems. Antiques, collectibles, and one-of-a-kind artworks beckon enthusiasts to uncover pieces that embody the island's creativity. In the lively atmosphere of St. James Market, every find becomes a story, a cherished memento that encapsulates the spirit of Trinidad and Tobago.

As travelers bid farewell to these captivating islands, the memories etched in their hearts are as diverse as the cultures that coalesce here. Whether it's the pulsating energy of Carnival, the savory delights of street food, or the tranquil beauty of Tobago's shores, Trinidad and Tobago beckon adventurers to return, to explore deeper, and to become part of the vibrant tapestry that makes these islands truly extraordinary.

In conclusion, Trinidad and Tobago are not just destinations; they are experiences that linger in the soul. The warmth of the sun, the echo of steelpan melodies, and the richness of cultural encounters create a symphony of memories that will resonate long after the journey ends. So, as the sun sets over the Caribbean horizon, we leave you with an invitation – an invitation to return, to discover anew, and to dance once more to the heartbeat of Trinidad and Tobago.

Printed in Great Britain
by Amazon

38978945R00056